At the Museum

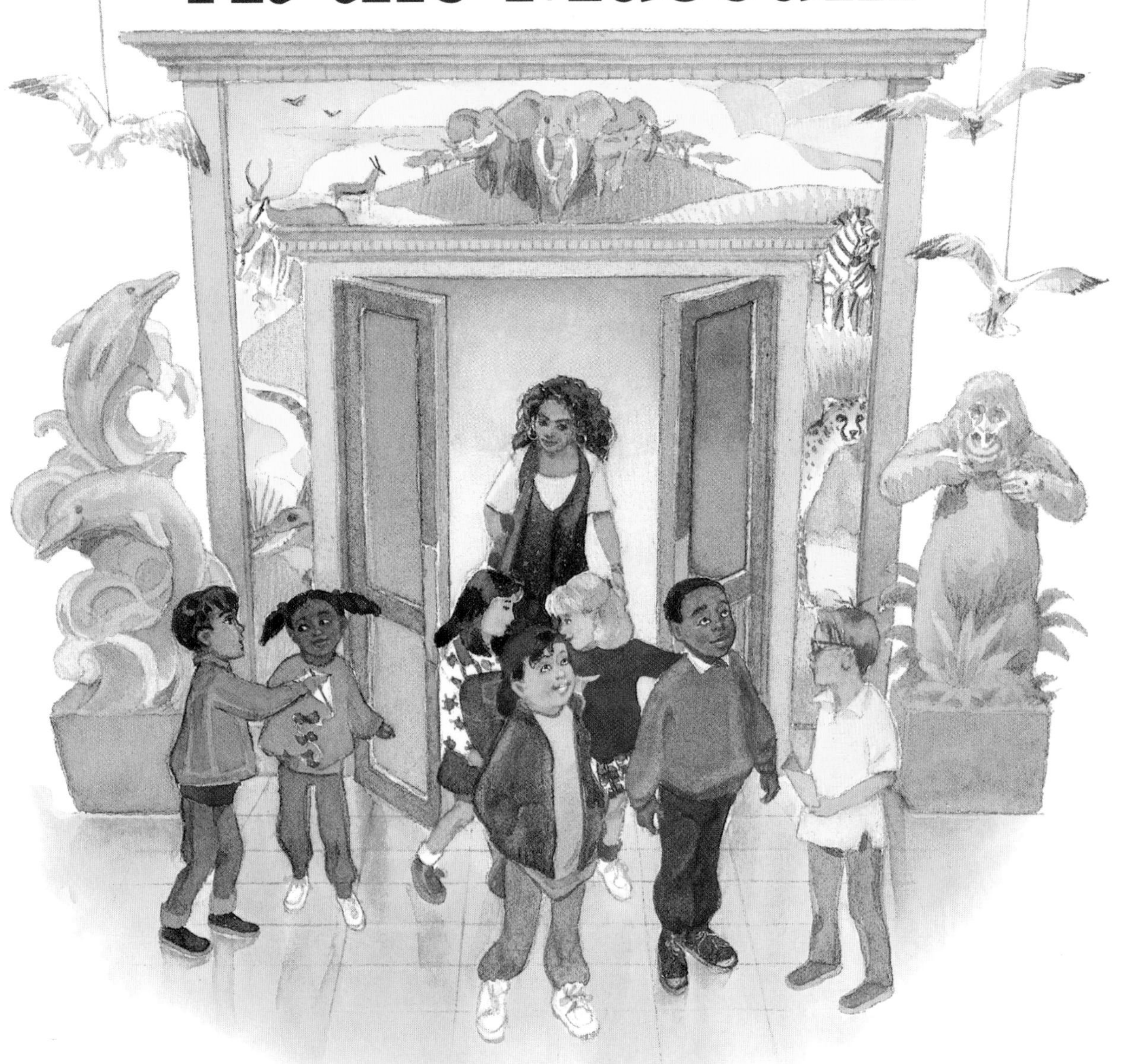

Written by Christine Economos

Illustrated by Joy Dunn Keenan

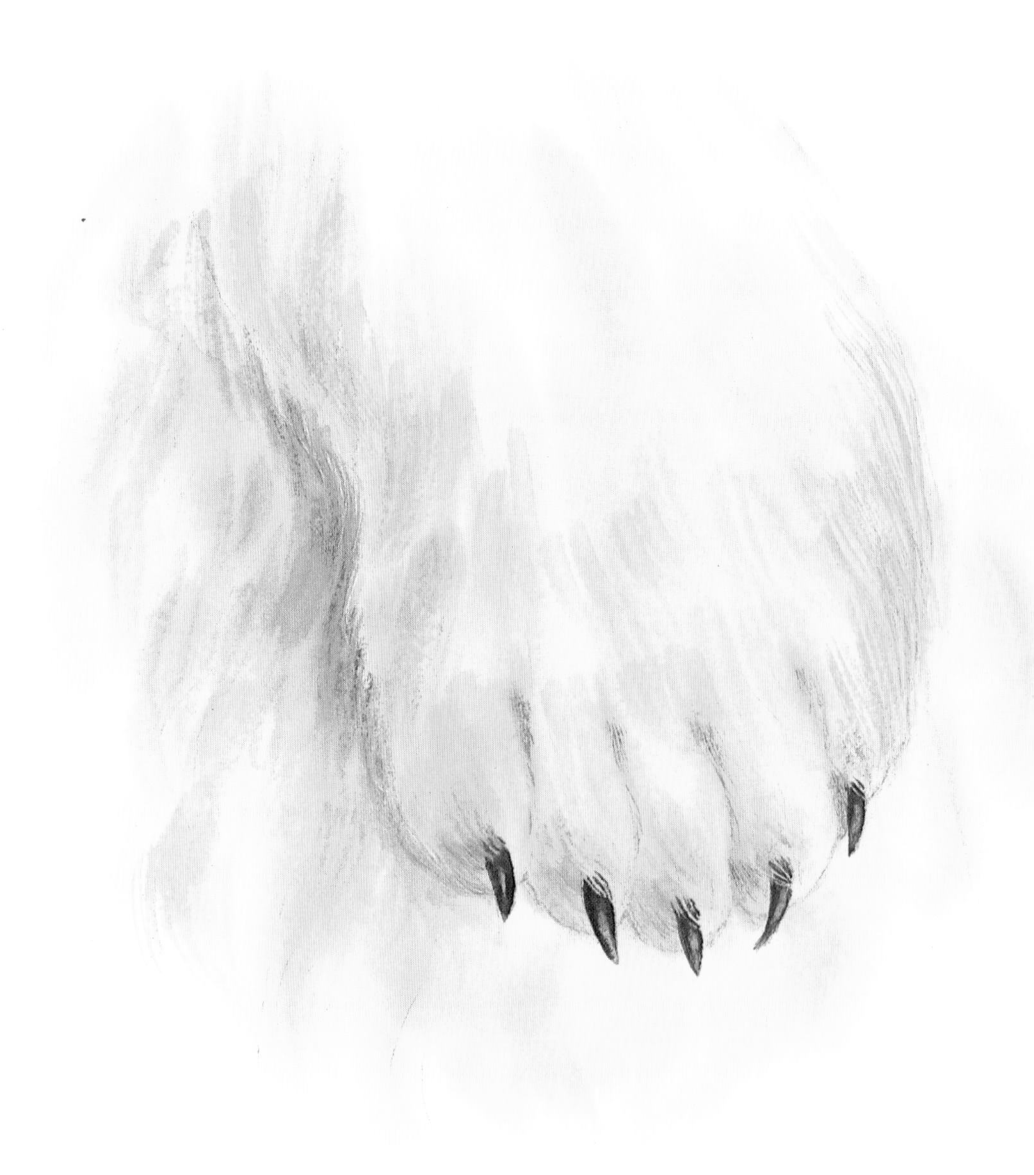

We saw a paw . . .

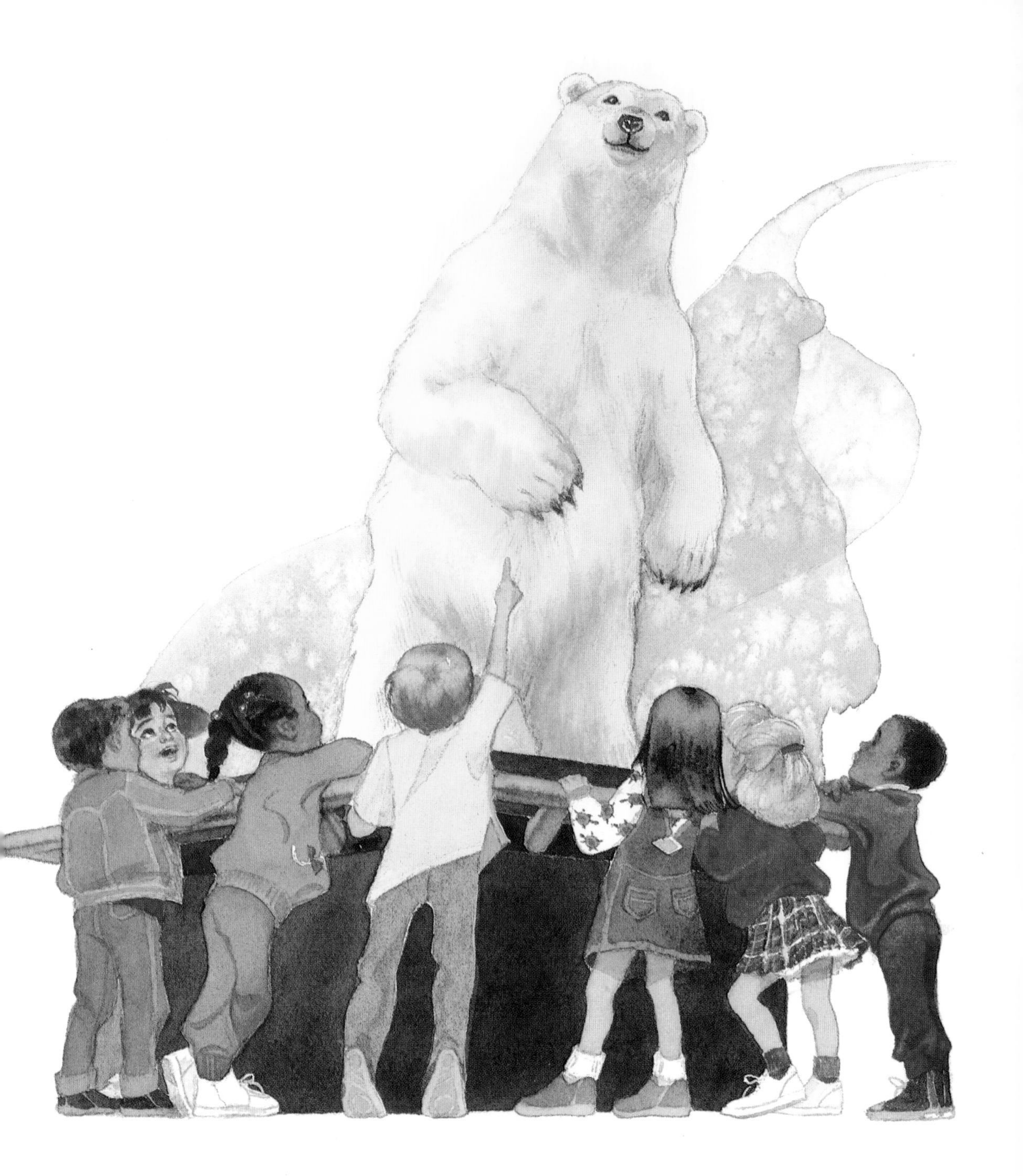

a very big paw!

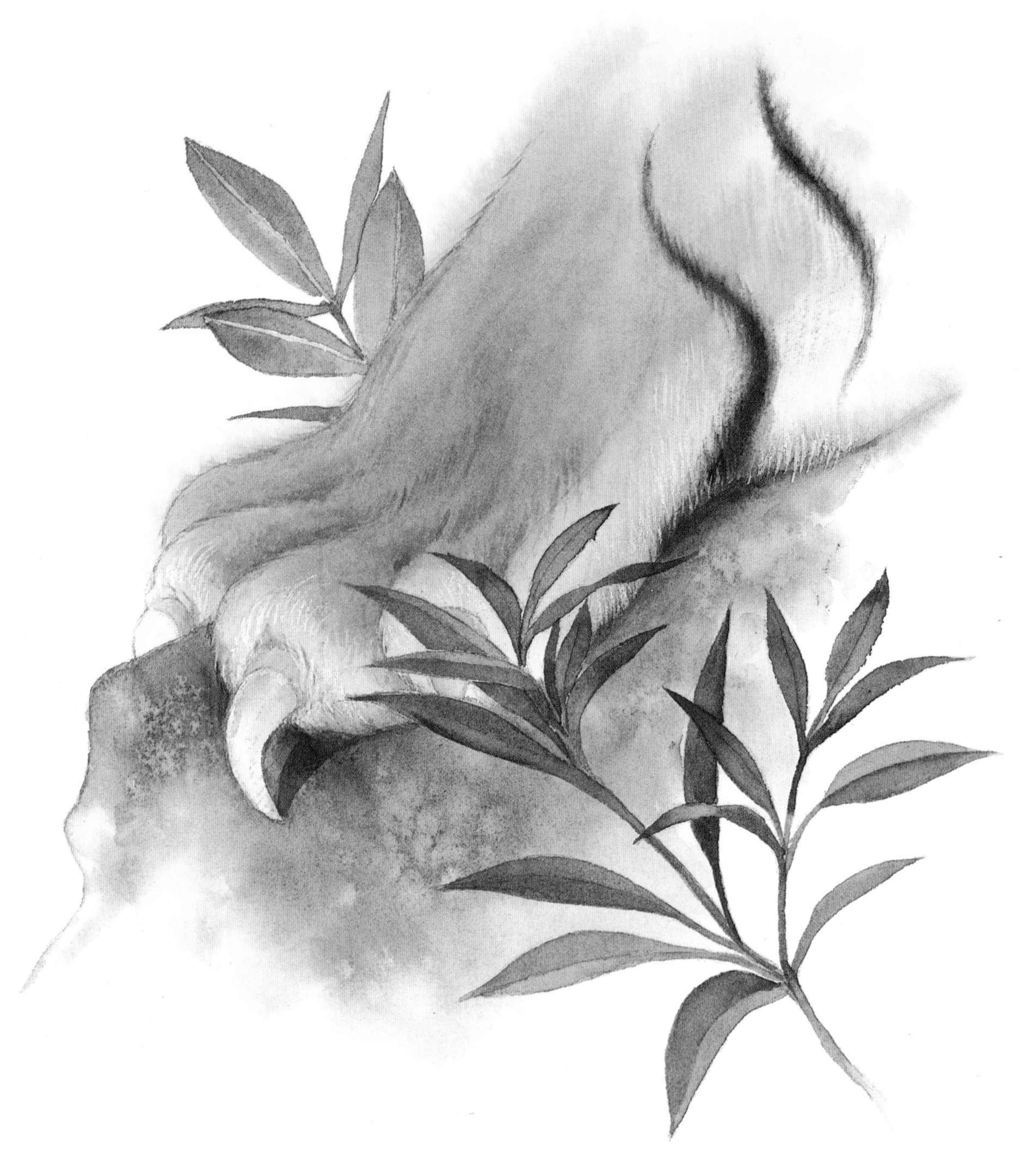

We saw a claw . . .

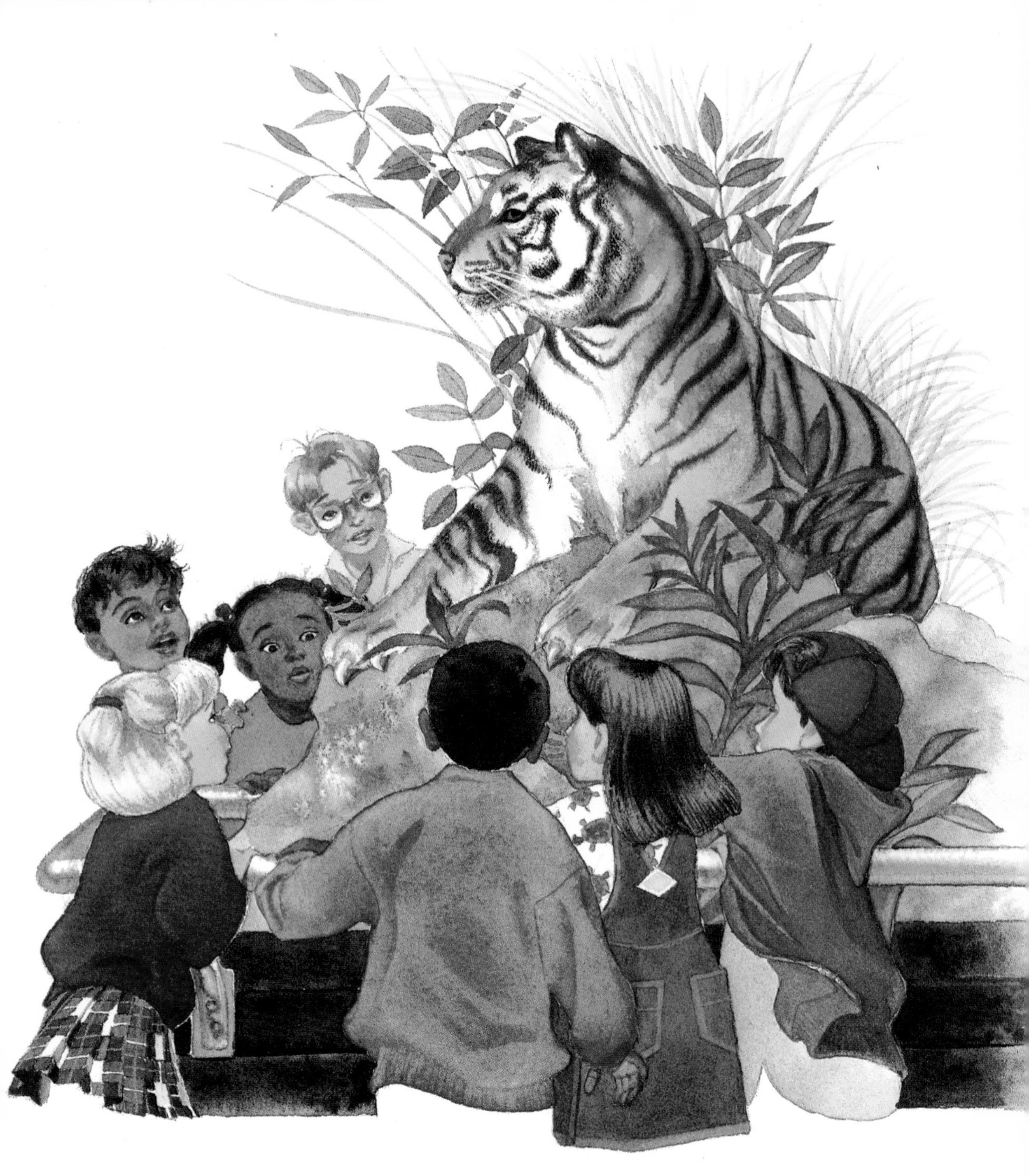

a very big claw!

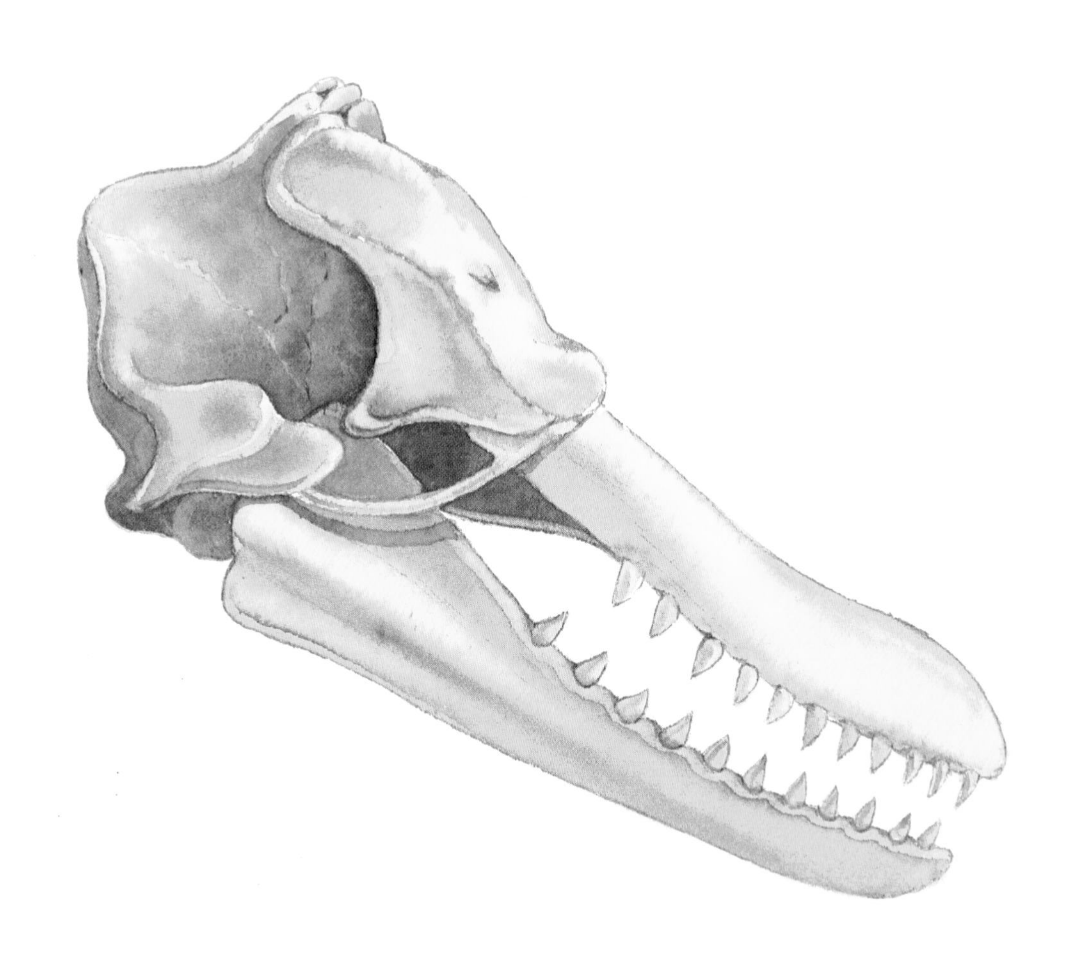

We saw a jaw . . .

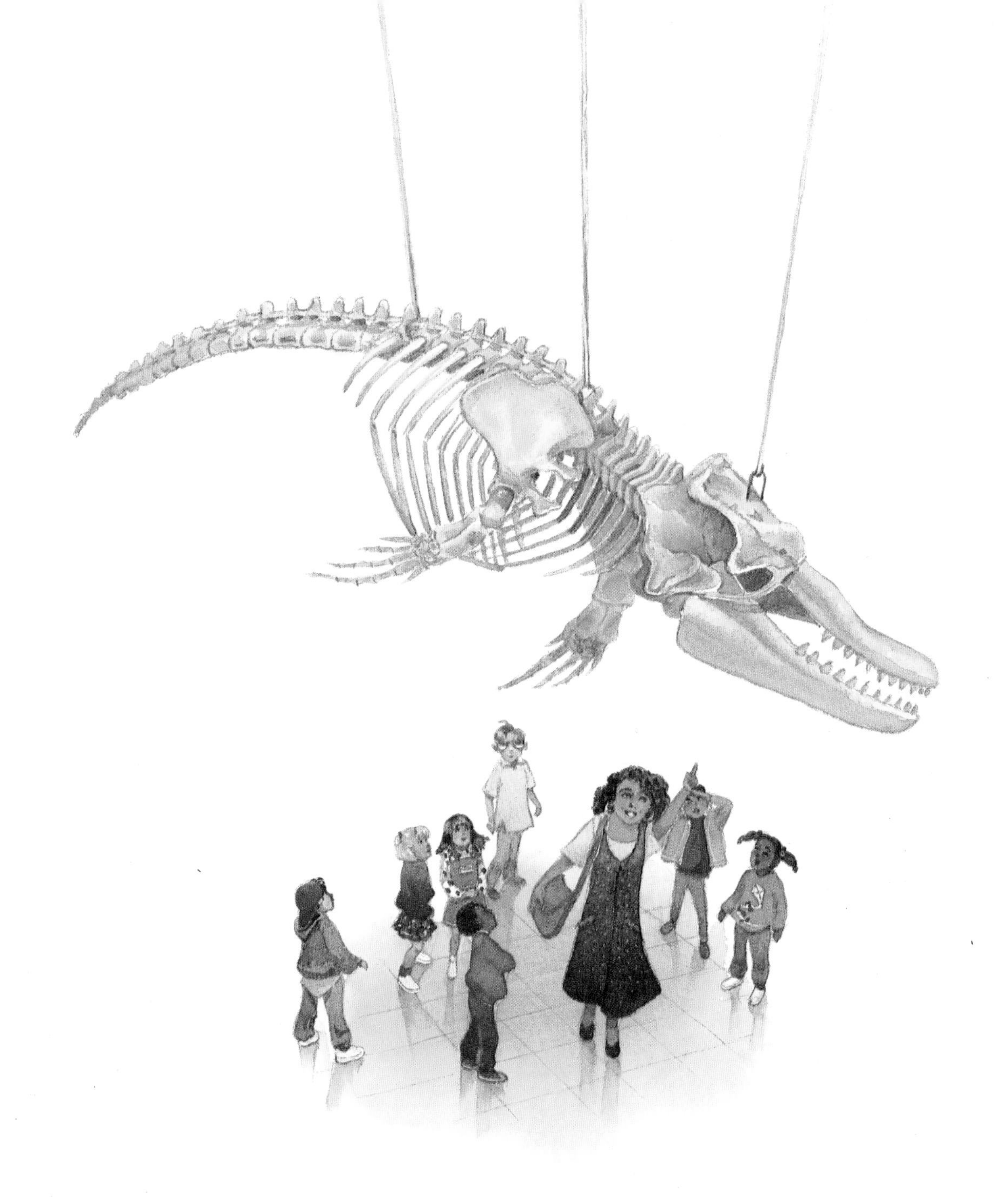

a very big jaw!

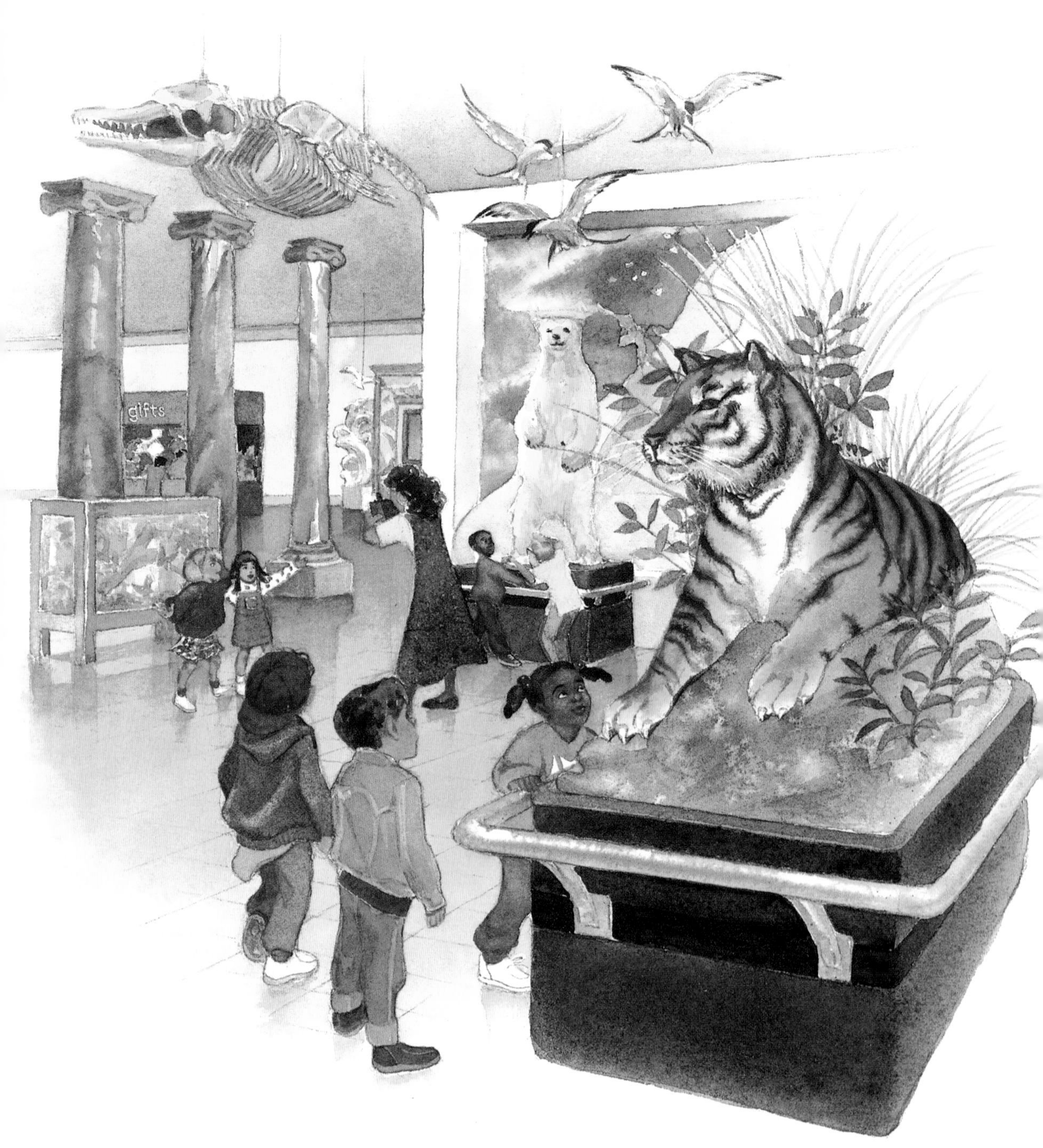

We saw it all!